50

WHISPERS IN THE WIND

WHISPERS IN THE WIND

MARTIN BUXBAUM

Illustrated by Kenneth Munn

THE WORLD PUBLISHING COMPANY
New York and Cleveland

Third printing, October 1970

© 1966 by Martin Buxbaum
All Rights Reserved

Library of Congress
Catalogue Card No. 65-23111

Printed in the U.S.A.

WORLD PUBLISHING
TIMES MIRROR

FOREWORD

Here are some small blossoms of verse
for your enjoyment, each having a different
meaning to each reader, depending
upon his own personal world

The drawings for it were made by Kenneth
Munn, a young graphic designer in
Washington, D.C.

Mr. Munn was chosen to do the art for the
1965 National Cherry Blossom Festival
Souvenir Program. *Whispers in the
Wind* was his first real venture into the
field of Japanese art.

The Japanese characters on the opposite page
spell out the title of the book.

Each day slowly shapes our lives
as dripping water
shapes the stone

If each blossom had a voice
we could not bear the sound of spring!

THE GARDEN POOL

Where one looks down to see the sky
and fish go swimming through the clouds

The voiceless mountains speak
of the eloquence that is in silence

Does mourning dove mourn just for me
Because I'm man, and he is free?

Shadows of the undone things
gather 'round my chair
and they silently reproach me
for the crown of dust I wear

WHILE
  I
    stand
      within
        the
          sunlight
others
  stand
    within
      the
        night.

Disease and flies and dusty skies
    and filth and mud and dirt
Bitter cold or sun that fries
    Hunger, anger, sweat and hurt
Endless labor . . . tomorrow, more
This is the world of the poorest poor

In a world where all is water
  who can tell when goldfish weep?

Hear the sighing of the forest
  buried 'neath the city's streets

Lightning shows its strength
by the fury of its stroke
and the acorn by its oak

There is but one time—the love-time
and all life begins in this season that is
   so different
in the each of us

THE DAYDREAMER

Bread cannot be made from roses
or wine from stars

IF Death were sweet as love can be
  and Paradise a certainty
tomorrow's sun but few would see

Whatever *my* mood
that is the mood
of the wind's song

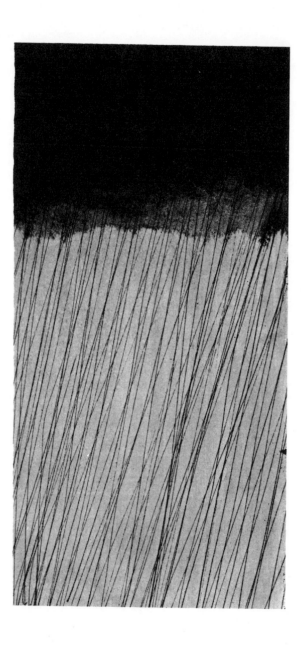

WOMAN—she speaks with the persistence
of rain

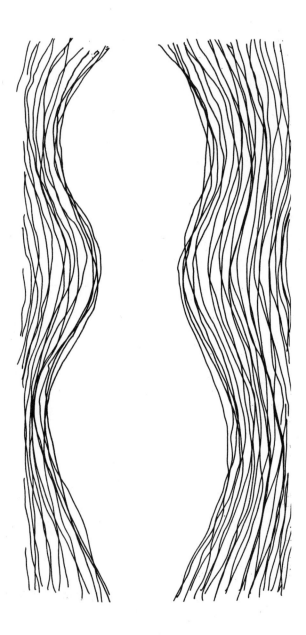

WHEN Adam found himself
in the Garden of Eden
he asked:
"Why, O, Lord, am I here?"
and when he saw woman
he knew.

The CHALICE

LOVE'S a chalice, made by two
   from fleecy clouds and morning dew
     of kisses by the fire's light
and whispers at the eve of night
   It's shaped with gentle, warm caress
     each time two lips together press

With care this wondrous thing could be
   theirs for an eternity
     but unkind words and glances mean
make the vessel lose its gleam
   and slowly chips away the core
     until the chalice
       is no more.

Nightingale is caged by bars
while man is caged on earth by stars

Day was meant for prayer and toiling
Night was meant for love and dreams

For such is the unbroken circle
   from the earth to the sky above
that to give of love is to give of life
   and in giving life, find love.

Nights
  I
    see
      his
          lanterns
              bobbing
I
  pretend
    he's
        plucking
          stars

Sometimes
　　life's
　　　not
　　　　what
　　　　　it
　　　　　　seems
as
　　sunlight
　　plucks
　　　　a
　　　　　sleeper's
　　　　　dreams

It is far safer
   to make friends with a lion
who believes in God
   than a mouse who doesn't

We were born crying
we must learn to laugh

THE ATOMIC BOMB

The dragon sleeps within his lair
yet all know that the Dragon's there

CONTRAST

O SAN built a house of beauty
   trimmed with gold and lacquer, red
In the shadow of its doorway
   Lim Po searched for crust of bread

O SAN always made his living
   from the gifts within his mind
Lim Po made his with his muscles
   like so many of his kind.

Weep not for the leaf of autumn
        as it brown and wrinkled lies
It has seen the rain in April
        and the pleasant summer skies

Only the Power can know the hour
   when a man must meet his God
For the space is brief 'twixt life and grief
   and the tryst with the waiting sod

CHILDREN—their world is so close
  I can touch it, and yet
their world is a lifetime away

風の囁き

God gave the gift of memory
    That I might close my eyes and see
The ones I love, and who love me.

FAITH is the warmth in the embers
when the firelight's died away

If only we
    could tell our fallen
        that the battle had been won!

When my stomach was full
   they called me Man
when empty
   they called me Beast

風の囁き

NOCTURNAL ARTIST

The mind at night
  freed from the rails
    of the workday world
      wanders where it will
        and paints its own pictures
       in dreams.

THE RETURN

The skull he held with practiced care
  once had fragrant lips and hair
    back when pyramids were young
      and praises to Osiris sung
The young man wondered, "Who was she?"
  but the ancient skull stared silently

Alone with it, his quiet room
   filled him with a nameless gloom
      He placed the skull with hollow eyes
         where sightless, it could face the skies
        and see the river, once again
still flowing, like an open vein

A wind rose, wailing, from the ground
   and filled the skull with sobbing sound
      through the mouth with twisted smile
        it seemed to form these words,
         "The Nile!"
           only this—then mournful sighs
         as woman makes, before
        she cries

He heard her soul's impassioned plea
   seeking what she could not see
      and carried her across the sand
        caressing her with tender hand
Down at the edge of river, green
   he placed the last of a Pharaoh's queen

Joined again, were the Nile and she
   it kissed her where her lips should be
      then drew her gently from the shore
        until she could be seen no more
and then he heard the river's foam
   whisper softly, "You are home!"

THE BLIND can find
   a world sublime
      the mute can talk
      the legless walk
      the deaf hear sound

ALL things are found
   within that wondrous world
      called MIND!

MAN, seeking Heaven
   someday finds
      that he walked through it
         many times
            without knowing
               until his memory tells him so.

HIS ANSWER

In each pinch of earth
   there are whole worlds
      and *no* man shall ever see
         the smallest of the small
            or the largest of the large
               of God's creations

And each living thing
   is a gospel unto itself
      ever mystifying man
         who eternally asks:
            "Is the seed more valued
               than the plant?"

Even if the Earth cried out
   "I gave you birth!"
      the Sun would answer:
         "You cannot bear a fragment of moss
            without me!"
               And yet another voice could
                  answer, saying:
                     "And where would *you* be
                        if My hand did not hold
                           you in orbit?"

For the sun each flower reaches
    Can not touch it—this they know
But this constant striving, reaching
    is what makes the flowers grow

Meditation upon The Lord's Prayer

OUR FATHER, of *all* living things
of every rock and tree
Hallowed be Thy very name
To speak, to write, to see
  Thy kingdom come, to everyone
  Within Thy universe
  Thy will be done, as sure as sun
  Shall morning sky traverse

Give us this day, our daily bread
to give us strength to serve
Forgive the sins we do each day
And all our good preserve

May we, as Thee, forgive the ones
Who do us wrong or harm
Guide us from temptation, with
Thy strong and gentle arm

Deliver us from evil, when
It enters in our heart
For goodness is *Thy* kingdom, and
We seek to be a part
Thine is the power! glory! Lord
And we are simply men
For ever guide us through this life
For ever, Lord—Amen.

HEAVEN

An angel stopped four men one day
　　And asked, "Pray tell me, what is Heaven?"
　　　　And each man answered differently
　　　　　　For each one in his mind could see
　　　　　　　　A Heaven that was made for him.

"Heaven," said the poet is
　　a place of warmth and sun
　　　　where birds and other things do play
wide meadow filled with flowers, gay
　　with drifting clouds upon its rim
　　　　"A house beside a little brook
well—visited by many friends
　　and not a single one unkind
　　　　"Work—to fill my hands and mind,
　　　　　　This, I would savor, to the brim!"

The warrior said, "Give me a sword!
　　a horse with fire within its eyes!
　　　　Then let me fight and not be slain
that I might live to fight again!
　　And many tales of battle spin!
　　　　"Let me hear the lusty yells
　　　　　　and other sounds of battle ring
and evenings laze around a fire
　　and drink of ale—this I desire
　　　　until eternity grows dim!"

"Give me a ship," the sailor cried,
   "with sail as white as a woman's throat
so I can stand upon the bow
   and feel the spray upon my brow!
      from here to land of Sanderkim!
"I'll glide through tropic, moonlit night
   and laugh at every screaming gale
      When tired of stroking the sea-cat's
         mane
I'll head for home and love again
   until the next sea's whim!

The Reverend sighed and raised his eyes
   "Heaven is to me," he said,
      "filled with many angels, fair
         and you can see God everywhere!
            in every cloud and hymn!
"There music of the seraphim
   fills the very air each day
      and there is an eternal peace
         where praises to Him never cease!
            This Heaven would I dwell within!

Each man had chosen Heaven that
   was made up of the things he loved
      and what he chose of greatest worth
         were all the things of mind or earth
eternity could never dim!
   For sky and home and battles large
      seas and ship and God and songs
are bits of Heaven given man
   that he might see in earthly span
      the Heaven *real* awaiting him!

THE MUTE

She had no voice
   and like a lovely flower
      needed none

Yesterdays are the petals
from the blossoms of Today
which grow from the seeds
of Tomorrow

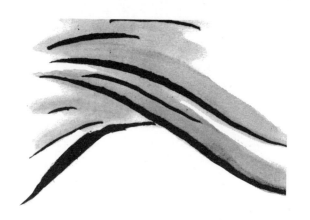

As seed falls on a barren stone
or drifts until it meets the sea
Only he will be alone
who deep within him wants to be

SOMEWHERE—out where the earth meets
    sky
        the last kiss will be kissed
            then die
        but not the final sigh
            'til we meet again—

Martin Ruxbaum